WRITE ON!

─│ON!│─

Idea-rich Tips and Techniques to bring your Book into Pixels or Print

BOB 'IDEA MAN' HOOEY
Author of Speaking for Success

WRITE ON! *Idea-rich tips and techniques to bring your book into pixels or print* **ISBN: 9781998014255**

Preface

"Writing is easy: Capture the thoughts, make the connections. The rest is editing."
Bob 'Idea Man' Hooey

I never intended being an author or a writer; a sad fact that my high school English assignments would prove. I loved to read but found myself struggling to capture my thoughts and to get my words to make sense on paper. It just seemed to be too-much-work for the lukewarm results and so-so responses to my early literary efforts.

Somewhere along the path things changed for me.

* Maybe it was the getting access to a typewriter where, when finished, I could *actually* read my scribbling.
* Maybe it was the getting a computer and learning I could brain dump my thoughts and come back later to re-arrange, edit, or even delete them.
* Maybe it was learning to organize my thoughts to successfully share my ideas and stories orally as a speaker; first in Toastmasters and, later, in the professional speaking arena as I travelled the globe.

In any case, I started writing and sharing my ideas in print (and later electronically) to find people enjoyed reading them and asked for more. When I first started down the path of professional speaking, I frequently had audience members ask, **"Do you have any books?"** *At the beginning, not a one. Later, I started asking them,* **"Why, would you buy one?"** *And their answer was,* **"Yes!"**

At the same time, I was gaining opportunities to share my writing as articles in North American consumer, corporate, association, on-line, and trade publications. This began slowly one publication at a time and some of my articles were picked up by numerous publications. Wow!

My articles, success tips, and innovative ideas on sales, leadership, career success, effective teams, presentation skills, and even writing (books) have been successfully applied by thousands of professionals around the world.

My choice to move into the realm of professional speaking did <u>not</u> originally include the concept of being an author. ☺

That bizarre idea never crossed my mind. But as I realized people were open to learn; I also realized that we needed to explore different avenues to allow them to learn.

So, I began to write more frequently. And, we started turning my writing into books and other products.

I began to hone my skills. I found it helped me in my speaking and in building a nice profitable and leveraged augment with our **Success Publications** boutique editing and publishing business with Irene.

Along the way I learned a few lessons, made connections to other authors who shared their lessons and coached me in my quest in this new endeavor. I'd love to share some of them with you, hence this little book. **WRITE ON my friends!**

Bob 'Idea Man' Hooey
www.ideaman.net
www.SuccessPublications.ca
bhooey@mcsnet.ca

"Effective writing communicates the message in a way that makes it easier for the reader to relate and react positively to what they (reader) understand. Effective writing is helped or enhanced by 'charting-a-course' to convey your message with impact."
Bob 'Idea Man' Hooey (Think before you Ink!)

Publishing a book can help you expand and enhance your business in 2020 and beyond. It can help differentiate you from your competition too! This can work in any industry!

Perhaps you've been told you need to write a book; to create physical or online products. This, 'they' tell you, will help you succeed, make lots of money, and even make you famous.

Perhaps? Perhaps NOT! ☺ We can help you explore whether this is a worthwhile investment of your time, expertise, and money.

Ever dreamed of being a best-selling author? Well, first you must write the book! We can help with that, and maybe the best-selling part too.

Depending on where you are in your writing journey you can have your new book published in as little as 30-90 days. Whether you are working on an article, a book, or creating one of a multitude of other Business Enhancement Success Tools (see Bob's BEST™) starting with the right questions provides a solid foundation for your success.

Bob has done different formats and lengths of his, in person, **NOW is the time! Authorship program**, for CAPS Chapters across Canada (Halifax, Ottawa, Montreal, Toronto, London) and one for NSA in Ft. Lauderdale, Fla.

We want you to be inspired and educated so you can move forward with your publishing project and see it successfully brought into the world. We drew from those events in creating this little guidebook, just for you!

Some areas to consider as you begin the writing process (consulting/coaching is available)

1. Selecting the best topic or theme to write about for a book. What do you *'actually'* know and love? Why not ask Canada's Ideaman for help in creating this for your work?

2. Creating an 'effective' title and tag line or sub-title. Taglines are sometimes even more important than a title. (See How to craft effective book titles and subtitles)

3. Getting the help, you 'need' to bring your book into reality: editors, proofreaders, graphic artists, etc. Ask Irene!

4. What to say about yourself – creating effective author bio's: Strategic sizzle sells.

5. Getting forewords, endorsements, reviews, and testimonials and why you need them. Endorsements are valuable!

6. Marketing your book online, choosing keywords that help you get noticed. Getting your friends to help create excitement and buzz. Returning the favour! We can even assist you in creating a customized webpage to showcase and sell your book. Again, Ask Irene!

7. Starting with the creative add-on business/product spin offs in mind – think in advance about other products that can be built around or from your book.

8. Why you should consider doing an e-pub, Smashwords, and kindle version as well as a print version at the same time.

9. Launching successfully – tips and techniques, and detours (leverage our experience and expertise).

10. How to run a best seller campaign – with a little help from your friends.

Proof reading

This is a critical piece in your publication. You can either enhance or detract from your brilliance based on the words and grammatical structure you use. We can ensure your publication has the most common mistakes eliminated so you put your best self forth in pixels and print. **See Proof reading marks** *(pdf)* Along with editing, this is a critical foundation for your future publication. *www.SuccessPublications\Pdfs\Proofreadingmarks.pdf*

Editing

This is where the real work begins. As Bob says, **"Writing is easy: Capture the thoughts, make the connections. The rest is editing."** Lots of editing. 😊

This is where the re-writing magic happens to tighten up your thoughts, refocus and clarify your ideas, and make sure it has a logical flow for the reader. See **Editing services are a foundation for successful publications by Irene Gaudet** *(pdf) www.successpublications.ca/Pdfs/EditingbyIreneGaudet.pdf*

Layout and Formatting

This is where your book takes shape as we help you sculpt it for easy reading. This where it gets formatted for uploading to print and/or epub or kindle versions. **What is the proper length for an e-book by Nina Amir** *(pdf)* *www.SuccessPublications.ca\Pdfs\Properlengthforanebook.pdf*

Cover Design

Creating an eye-catching cover is a crucial part of your publishing process. This where you design a cover that catches the reader's eye and entices them to pick up or order your book. We can help you with this part of the process and recommend *cost-effective* designers as needed to bring it to life.

Kindle, Amazon, and Smashwords submissions

We have lots of experience in each of these avenues. We can help you submit your new 'baby' to these book sites.

Distribution

In addition to Smashwords, Kindle, and Amazon around the globe, you can get your book listed with on-line companies such as Barnes and Noble, iTunes and others. Ask us to help you handle this or coach you through it.

Promotion

Once you've published, then what? Creating buzz, maybe a best seller campaign, and generally getting the word out is important to making your work worthwhile.

 **PRO Tip: Tips on working with a professional proof-reader and editor by Irene Gaudet www.vitrakcreative.com**

A proof-reader is an **absolute** necessity as you will need another set of eyes on your copy. We often miss glaring errors as we see what we thought we wrote, not necessarily what is on the page. Don't feel insulted if your manuscript comes back with a lot of corrections needed. We all miss things, and the proof-reader is only trying to make yours a better product! Find someone you can trust to clean up the obvious problems without imposing their style upon your writing. That can be a fine line and ensure that changes do not lose your specific 'voice' in your publication.

An editor, on the other hand, may do a more massive assessment of your copy and ask for re-writes or edits. They will point out flaws in your content and layout. For both services, you will usually have to submit part of your manuscript to get an estimate of the costs you will incur.

Hard and fast rule of successful publications: Never, never, never let anything go into print virtually or in real life without having it at the very least proof-read!

Proofreading services: You need to have one last pair of eyes to read through for corrections before publication. Have your (free or paid) proof-readers **check your manuscript for:**

1. Spelling errors and consistent spelling (blond vs. blonde and toward vs. towards)
2. Doubled words
3. Missing words
4. Homophones (there vs. their)
5. Missing or incorrect punctuation
6. Proper formatting for e-book and/or print editions

Copy editing services: These include grammar, spelling, and basic sentence structure, style, and clarity for your readers. This will be something you can contract with a professional.

1. Correcting errors listed under proofreading
2. Consistent style throughout
3. Insure people, places, and things remain consistent throughout (if a novel)
4. Check for redundancy: Repetitive passages
5. Sentence clarity and wordiness:
   • Awkward sentences
   • Grammar (except where grammar "errors" are part of the author's style)

Content editing services- which includes plot, narrative characterization, flow, believability. More appropriate for a novel but might still be applicable for a non-fiction book.

1. Character history and development
2. Logical plot movement and development
3. Search for sections that do not move the plot forward and slow the story
4. Balance between scenes, narrative, action, and dialogue

Becoming a writer…

My transition to author and speaker radically changed my concept of being an effective communicator.

I still remember my mom reading through my fourth book (**Speaking for Success – now in its 9th edition, 2020**). I sat on the couch, expectantly, watching her read intently and making approving sounds. When she at last put it down, she looked at me and with a funny smile asked, *"Where did you learn to do this? We never saw this skill in high school!"*

- Truth is, perhaps it wasn't there or perhaps my writing was so un-readable that it (talent or skill) went unnoticed.
- Another point, back then, I had to write on topics chosen by others. Motivation is a big factor in effective writing!
- Now, I get to write what moves me, what comes from the passion inside, and what comes from a place of helping people become more productive or successful. That choice brings a freedom and a freshness to my words.

Oh, did I mention my mom was a retired English teacher. She used to send back my letters, corrected… in red ink.

I loved my mom, and it was an interesting experience to live long enough to see that look of amazement and pride on her face. I will miss her gentle correction and guidance. I dedicate every book I write to her to honor her memory and investment in my life. My wife, Irene has taken on this role.

"A short story must have a single mood and every sentence must build towards it." **Edgar Allen Poe**

Publish or Die? The product/publishing problem…

I have been in the field of professional speaking, coaching, and training for well over 25 years. As professional speakers and service providers, many of us struggle with the 'product problem'. Very similar to other businesses and industries. ☺

Many of us have been told we need a book or that a book will supercharge our careers and get the phone to ring off the wall. That challenge and the mixed results can leave us confused and at times disillusioned. **Books and other products can be a valued addition to our business and our audiences.**

I would like to offer a few ideas on my experiences and challenges overcome in this area. There are **three areas to cover: the concept, the creation, and the completion of the sale of our books and products.**

This section was originally an article for a national magazine that primarily focused on ideas nudging my fellow professional trainers, facilitators, and keynote speakers. However, it has direct **relevance for any industry professional seeking to add or enhance their value to potential clients.**

This concept works well in the development of training tools to assist or equip your team and organization to succeed. **But first you must ask:**

- **What do I know?**
- **What can I do?**
- **What can I provide that would add additional value?**

Valid questions to evaluate and enhance your career and business. They work for non-profit organizations as well as governmental and corporate ventures.

"Never use a long word where a short one will do."
George Orwell

Let me ask you: **Why would you want to have a book, publication, or product available?** Here were some of my answers when I asked myself that question. Perhaps, they will offer some hints in your own quest. **Ask yourself?**

DO:
- I believe in my topic and want to help reinforce my sessions with helpful take-home-tools?
- I want to build another stream of income to augment my speaking and training (or business) income?
- I want to establish and expand my credibility as an expert in my areas of study? This applies in many arenas/industries.
- I want to have something that will provide cash flow at my non-paid presentations.
- I want to assist my clients to become more informed prior to them making good buying decisions. Gee, this sounds like sales in many business ventures, doesn't it?
- I want to have something to use as a promotional tool to define what I do and differentiate myself from my competition? Branding and top of mind awareness can be enhanced in any business when you are featured 'in print'!
- I want to sharpen my thinking, focus my efforts, and deepen my expertise?
- I want to add value to my retail or service business. I did that when I was designing kitchens by writing and self-publishing **"How to remodel your kitchen and stay married!"**
- All the above?

If you answered **YES** to any of these, you are on the right track. Each of these is a valid reason for putting effort into developing a book or product in your business.

Ask my CAPS colleague, **Harold Taylor**, CSP about his commitment to develop at least one new product every 6 months. *(even in his 'retirement')*

But how do I do that you ask?
And where do I start?

Here are some suggestions on products, or as I now call them
Bob's B.E.S.T. (Business Enhancing Success Tools ™):

- Tip sheets and paper forms
- Booklets and pamphlets
- Manuals and workbooks
- E-books and e-publications *(Kindle, Smashwords, Nook)*
- Pocket Wisdom books
- Print books and anthologies (co-authored with others)
- Special reports and monographs *(sometimes called mini-books – I've done a whole series)*
- Resource guides
- Motivational posters and buttons
- Collections of articles – in book or e-pub format
- Sales, speech, time, and management planners or tools
- Video recordings – **YouTube** *(growing right now)*
- DVD videos and training programs
- Paid subscription newsletters or e-zines
- Software and apps
- Co-op products with other speakers and business providers

These ideas are value-added tools in any business arena!
Where can you create these to help yourself in yours?

Check out these ideas to kick-start your back of room and
passive income sales.

- If you ask you might get a free video shoot. My close friend and fellow past CAPS-Vancouver President, **Greg Gerrie** spoke for a special fee a few years ago and received a full professional video recording of the event. *I did that last year (2019) when I spoke in Manila. As well, I take advantage of opportunities to purchase videos like my session in Paris.*

- Starting in 2006, while doing work for a large Canadian Retailer, I accessed their film studio and crew to produce a series of short videos, which I was then able to re-use for other purposes. *Many of them are still in use today.*
- Invest in a digital tape and/or video recorder and record all your presentations. At the very least, you can capture video clips for YouTube and your website.
- Put together a collection of your motivational sayings and other quotes. (E.g. Sell a series of 12 done on parchment.) *We did that with our Secret Selling Tips series.*
- Take your handouts or 'learning guides' and turn them into monographs, pamphlets, manuals, or workbooks. That is how I got launched in writing and publishing.

Early in my speaking and training career, I did some work for a local Vancouver, BC college. They offered to 'print' my workbook and **'pay me $15 for each student'** for the privilege. **Wow!** This printing fee motivated me to get off my butt and start converting my 'free' handouts into licensable work and to produce workbooks, manuals, and books that I continue to sell.

Remember the folks who used to ask me if I had a book? Well, now I did, and they started buying them. Still do!

My friend and Past National CAPS President, **Jeff Mowatt**, CSP, HofF put together a series of articles for sale that generate sales for his recordings. Add sales of individual articles in your catalogue or convert into monographs or pamphlets.

A speaker friend from Calgary, **Alice Wheaton** took her course material on cold calling, broke it down into smaller pieces, and developed a series of smaller booklets. *Very similar idea to my mini-book series.*

Flesh out your product line by referencing other books (*especially fellow CAPS/NSA/GSF members*) in your talks and have some of them available as point of purchase and on your product list or catalogue. Most speakers and publishers will give you anywhere from 25% - 50% off retail for your own sales.

Ok, so now I've developed some products, but I'm not comfortable selling from the platform. How can I entice my audiences to purchase these *'treasures'?*

I still struggle with selling from the platform; but let me share these ten ideas I have found valuable.

1) Have a **display table** at the front of the room located in plain sight of your audience when you are speaking. Let your audience become *visually familiar* with it. Bonus: this adds to your platform credibility too. *For some reason authors who speak generate more credibility.*

2) While presenting, subtly pick up a book, or relevant product and quote or read ***directly*** from it. This increases visibility and acts as a subliminal enticement to look at, and often purchase the book or product you shared.

3) I frequently give away at least one of my books to a member of the audience. As the person is coming up, I tell them about their choice (from 4 or so). *This is a 'subtle' commercial without being too obvious.*

4) When speaking for an association or non-profit group, I will ask them to handle sales and then donate a portion of each sale. Often, they become better salespeople than my own efforts, and tell the audience about the donation, which spurs sales.

5) When speaking for a corporate or professional group, I have been following a tip of having some of my products at the table and allowing people to simply pick them up and drop a cheque or cash in the box. *Surprisingly, this self serve, honour system has worked well for me too.*

6) Now that I have quite a few books, a Pocket Wisdom series, an equal number of resource guides, and special reports, (and more on the way) I am doing some packaging deals (Success systems) for my audiences. And it is working! *Challenge your creativity and make it easy for them to buy.*

7) Develop an order form or catalogue with your products. Have it available on the product table, or better yet as part of your learning guide or handouts for distribution to everyone who attends. I have my own **B**usiness **E**nhancement **S**uccess **T**ools mini catalogue. **I include a listing of my current publications at the end of each one.** It is also available on-line for information and ordering from my main web site. Visit **www.ideaman.net** We have an online store to cover print and e-copy publications as well: **www.SuccessPublications.ca**

8) Send the order form or catalogue along with any order or enquiry you get from potential clients. Don't be afraid to show your proficiency and expertise in print and on-line! *This can generate repeat excitement and new business!*

9) Have some product information listed on your evaluation form. My colleague, the late, **Dottie Walters**, CSP taught me this one. You'd be surprised at how this can generate interest and post-presentation sales.

10) Mention your publications and products in your interviews, articles, and other promotional materials such as speaker bio or by-lines. Don't be afraid to include copies of relevant product with your promo package. I had a call from a Montreal based firm about some Customer Service training and sent along my C/S DVD and a book. We're now exploring some long-term work together across North America. On-line for now and LIVE post Covid-19.

Following 9-11, the 2008 economic meltdown, and again since Covid-19, I have been re-evaluating what I am doing in my speaking and training business. More effective use of product as both a promotional and profit generation tool is starting to play a valuable part in my ongoing growth in this industry.

My challenge to you is – what is your next step? It may be essential for you and your team to grow. Some of these ideas may be a nice fit to expand or enhance your business.

If I can do it, why can't you?

What kind of '*product*' can you design and deliver that will help your audiences, team members, your clients, or your organization? Do you have a book burning inside you?

Bob's note: It is too easy for those around you, who are hopelessly mired in their own mediocrity, to criticize you for trying to follow your dream, write your great novel, become a more effective writer, or acting to implement your great idea.

Theodore Roosevelt, who was often criticized, wrote: *"...it is not the critic who counts, not the man who points out how the strong man stumbled, or where the doer of deeds could have done them better. **The CREDIT belongs to the man (or woman) who is actually in the arena, who strives valiantly - who knows the great enthusiasm, the great devotion ... and spends himself (or herself) in a worthy cause.** Who at best, knows the triumph of high achievement; and at the worst, if he (or she) fails ... at least fails while daring greatly, so that his (or her) place shall never be with those cold and timid souls ... who know neither victory nor defeat."*

A final word, **"Remember, they don't build monuments to critics"** Bob 'Idea Man' Hooey

PRO-TIP: Using dialogue in your writing – fiction or non-fiction

"If you're using dialogue, say it aloud as you write it. Only then will it have the sound of speech." John Steinbeck, Pulitzer Prize winner and Nobel Laureate. Author of *Grapes of Wrath* and *Of Mice and Men*

Adding dialogue between characters in your novel or even your business success masterpiece adds energy, interest and makes your book more readable and relevant. Look for ways to introduce stories, with dialogue, into your flow to keep your readers' interest and to make what you say more impactful. *I work to make my writing conversational and interesting.*

'Your book' can be so-much-more than 'just a book'

- It can be an effective business card and brochure
- It can become your salesforce to reaching new clients
- It can be an introduction to new people
- It can be an introduction to enhanced media exposure
- It can become a profitable business in itself
- It can be your own personal fund raiser
- It can be a launch point for a cause you truly support
- It can be the source of increased cash flow
- It can be the beginning of a new business empire
- It can allow you to share your heart with strangers
- It can be the source of increased visibility and credibility
- It can be a source of passive long-term income
- It can become your core brand
- It can be your written voice in connecting with new clients
- It can be a major boost to your personal & professional confidence
- It can be an effective way to export your message
- It can support and enhance your true calling
- It can be a dream come true - yes it can happen to you!
- It can allow you to spend more time with your family
- It can be a process to help you grow and succeed.
- It can also be a source of personal/professional pride.

But, you say…

- **I don't** know how to write
- **I don't** have the time to write
- **I don't** have the expertise to edit
- **I don't** know how to publish it

- **I don't** know how to format/layout
- **I don't** have the discipline
- **I don't** have the confidence

You don't have to navigate these alone, WE can help:

- **We can help** you organize your thoughts to write
- **We can teach** you how to carve out writing time
- **We can be** your in-house publishing experts
- **We can guide** you through the whole publishing process
- **We can do** that just for you
- **We can be** your accountability partner
- **We can be** your motivational coaches
- **We can be your dream achievement team**

In short, we (Success Publications) are committed to helping you succeed in getting your brilliance out in both pixel and print formats. **Call us! +1-780-736-0009 or drop us an email: Bob bhooey@mcsnet.ca** or Irene **igaudet@mcsnet.ca**

"If it sounds like writing, I rewrite it." Elmore Leonard

Communication basics

In life, more so in business, we have numerous opportunities and responsibilities to effectively share our ideas. As leaders in business or the community, our success, and perhaps our survival, is directly dependant on our ability to do so quickly and productively. As authors, even more so.

In this section, we will focus primarily on the written form of communication. However, since business is more than just writing, we will also be touching on some tips on listening skills and the art of presentation skills these comparisons and differences should be noted as we begin.

3 basic forms of communication:

Oral communication
- Presentations – sales, board meetings, customer, training
- Meetings – training, sales, team
- Informal talks – staff, management, clients
- Interviews – client, potential employees
- Telephone calls – sales calls
- Voice mail messages

Written communication
- Letters and memos
- Reports and books
- Business cards
- Brochures and promotional literature
- Websites
- Articles
- Faxes
- Emails
- E-books
- Internet business
- Other forms of written materials

Non-verbal communication
- Body language
- Dress
- Personal grooming

I've heard it said that **"Communication is two-way understanding."** Makes you think!

Perhaps**, 'Oral communication is two-way listening'.**

Following that logic, **'Written communication is two-way reading'.**

And finally, **'Non-verbal communication is two-way seeing.'**

What do you think? Perhaps it is the effective use of all three that results in the understanding between two people called communication.

Getting your point across – making the connection!

1. **Convey your message** and ideas clearly, completely, quickly, and with confidence.
2. **Present your message** or information from the listener or reader's point of view.

Purpose determines Path

Being clear about your purpose will assist you in choosing the most effective communication path to convey your message accurately and productively. This is where you set course for success!

- Do you want to speak directly, meet in person, or convey your message in written form?
- What is your purpose in each case?

Here are a few examples:

Using the direct approach such as the telephone, Zoom, Skype, or Messenger might be the best choice for these types of situations:

- I need information and I need it immediately or today! Speed is a factor?
- Here is the answer to the question you asked, or here is the information you requested.
- I think we need to discuss or clarify this situation. Or, I need some additional information or some direction to be able to continue.
- I need two-way interaction and want your help.
- I need to hear your voice and or see you to assess your commitment.
- I'd like to make an appointment to follow up on this in person.

Writing might be the better choice in these instances:

- When the addition of a written format will strengthen your oral presentation.
- Will it make a greater impact?
- Do you need documentation or tracking on a project or proposal?
- Will a carefully crafted memo convey the message effectively?
- Do you have the time to put it in writing?
- Do I have information to present to more than one person?

Calling a meeting might be beneficial if:

- You need two-way communication or interaction from other people. (2020 – think Zoom)
- You have information to present to more than one person.

- What needs to be communicated requires a more formal format?
- See other information we've provided on meetings, if you feel this is the best way to go. Visit our website: **www.ideaman.net** for more information on how to create and host a successful meeting.

More thoughts on purpose

Whether you are planning an oral presentation or working on something in a written format doing your homework and defining your purpose is critically important. This is where you **'THINK before you ink!'** (visit www.SuccessPublications.ca to purchase your personal copy)

It will help you more effectively convey your message and, as a bonus, assist you in the structure, research, and delivery too.

What is your objective?

- Do you want to make a request?
- Do you want to convey information?
- Do you want to call someone to action?
- Do you want to bring a problem to their attention?
- Do you want to bring an opportunity to their attention?
- Do you have a recommendation to make?
- Are you trying to sell your abilities, services, or programs?
- Do you want them to commit to a course of action?
- Do you want to entertain them? Amuse them?
- Is it your intent to present a convincing argument?
- Do you seek to inspire or motivate them?
- Do you want their feedback and input?
- Do you want to keep them in the loop?
- Do you report to them?
- Do they report to you?
- Are you colleagues or equals in responsibilities and scope?

Identify your audience's preference

- Do they like to *'read'* this type of material, or would they prefer to *'see or hear'* it? Ask them or ask those close to them about their preferences. Then deliver it accordingly.
- Are they interested in numbers, cost benefits, investment, techniques and tips, background, or people?
- Are they conservative in their views and actions? Are they more progressive in their background and viewpoint?
- Are they easy or difficult to convince? What is their track record?
- How much time can they realistically be expected to allocate to this presentation?
- Are you competing in this situation with another firm, another colleague, time deadlines, cost factors, and market pressure?
- Who are they? Professional vs. non-professional, or personal? What is your relationship to them?
- What else do you know about them?

Taking the time to do this additional homework will assist you to make better use of your organization, preparation, and delivery time. It will help you deliver it in a format that will allow your message to gain a better reception and perhaps acceptance.

You'll be closer to the mark in your efforts and minimize your risk by delivering a well thought out and crafted presentation – either verbal or written.

A quick review
- Why would you want to take the extra time and effort it takes to make an effective presentation?
- What would it accomplish?

"Quantity produces quality. If you only write a few things, you're doomed." **Ray Bradbury**

 **PRO-Tip: If you are writing an article or book, "Who is your reader?" Craft your thoughts and write for that person!**

Like the key question in business, **"Who is your ideal client"**, having a reader in mind will help you structure and craft your book for maximum impact and readability.

- Who are they? Age? Sex? Occupation? Marital status? Education? Dreams? Life experiences? Community involvement? Etc.?
- What do they care about? Concerned about?
- What do you know that would be of benefit or solve a problem for them?

Ideas on how and where to promote your book or group in your community

Here are a few ideas on how you can actively promote your book, group, organization, or personal activities in your community. These ideas are focused more on the private sector but would work with a few creative twists for public and personal efforts too. **Some will work for a book promotion.**

LOCAL NEWSPAPERS may be the easiest way to secure media coverage, as they are traditionally more accessible than radio and TV stations. Additionally, being print media, they often allow you to communicate more information than other media. And they are often 'looking' for local news events and activities. *You need a hook, not just you wrote a book!*

BROADCAST MEDIA are also a great source of promotion with public service announcements (PSA's) which might be video-taped or scripted for their on-air use.

I've found the local cable companies quite receptive as well as the local radio and TV PSA listings.

You might investigate offering your services to a local talk show as a guest or host, if you have an interesting twist or newsworthy idea to share. **Use your book as a credibility tool to open your conversations.** It never hurts to try and the worse they can say is no!

CHAMBERS OF COMMERCE can be a great connection for promotion of your book, cause, company, or community group and for personal networking. An advertisement or announcement in their newsletter or directory can be both effective and inexpensive. As a member, you can obtain a membership list and do some selective broadcast faxing or direct mail work. *I've done that successfully over the years.*

Offer to speak on your area of expertise and become a value-added resource for them. I've done this for years and found it to be a great way to gain recognition and local exposure. If you publish a newsletter/book, make sure your local library gets a couple of copies for their business reference section.

LIBRARIES will often allow you to post flyers and announcement on their bulletin boards. If you are a service group or provider let them know who you are and what you do.

They often get calls for information and can refer people to you or your group. If you publish a newsletter, make sure your local library gets a couple of copies for their reference section. If you get extra copies of industry periodicals, have **written a book or some other publication, I'd suggest donating a copy.**

POLITICS: You might even decide to throw your hat in the ring for public office. You may not win, but you certainly get exposure. Many years ago, in New Westminster I ran a fun **'Bob the Bear for Mayor'** campaign to encourage people to get out and vote. I didn't win, but the positive press including front-page picture and story didn't hurt my business (a cute little coffee shop on main street.) *Think book promotion!*

IN HOUSE PUBLICATIONS are often looking for material and submissions o interest to their readership. Public, private and association publications are actively looking for good materials to use. I what you do or know can be structured in such a way as being informative and interesting for their readers, you have a great chance of getting published.

I've had articles published across North America and the globe from this simple activity and some of them have resulted in business for my speaking and facilitation services. Contact their editors about submission deadlines, areas of interest and editorial style. Ask about submitting 'fillers.' Fillers are articles of various lengths that are generic, timeless in focus and can be used when needed. You might be surprised at the results.

Note: I offer a series of free downloadable business enhancing articles on various topics on my website. Visit us at: www.ideaman.net to access

LOCAL CHURCHES can help in passing on information to their members if what you offer is of interest or helpful to them. Let them know what you offer, and how you might be of assistance to their congregations. *Perhaps your book would fit.*

COLLEGES, UNIVERSITIES, or INSTITUTES may have internal cable TV networks or radio broadcast facilities. *When I attended the U of A (in another life) I was program director for CKSR Student Radio and did my own show every Friday morning where I interviewed people in addition to playing music.* Also, check out their student publications, newspapers, staff newsletters and electronic media. If you are a knowledgeable speaker on your topic, you might be invited to be a guest lecturer on a related discipline. For years, I promoted my kitchen design business and cabinet sales by doing guest visits to the architectural and design departments of a local Tech.

It built credibility, gave me an increased sense of self-confidence, and drew new clients as well. You may be able to participate in career days or other related events held on campus.

PRIVATE TRAINING COLLEGES OR TRADE SCHOOLS can also be a good source of contact to promote your event or organization. They too, are looking for knowledgeable **guest authors** who might be willing to share them from their expertise and professional experiences.

ALLIED BUSINESSES, COMMUNITY GROUPS OR SERVICE PROVIDERS Take a moment and investigate the possibilities of working co-operatively in marketing or promotional efforts. Group efforts can work wonders! Find out what they offer to the community, or if you have compatible or non-competitive services or products, or if you have common areas of concern, or services. See if they will agree to combine marketing or public relation efforts. Join efforts could be the best use of time, resources, and personnel, with a benefit to both parties.

INTERNET: I have been promoting my books on Facebook and LinkedIn… in fact, recently. I shared one publication (***SUCCEED! Idea-rich strategies to succeed in business despite global disruptions***) to more than 28 million people via my LinkedIn groups. I have also been interviewed numerous times on-line on one of my books. Get yours here: ***www.successpublications.ca/SUCCEED!.pdf***

CO-OP: Co-operative promotion with other authors… this works and in fact this is how so many authors find their books hitting, even if briefly, best seller status on Amazon.

"There is nothing to writing. All you do is sit down at a typewriter and bleed." **Ernest Hemingway**

PRO-Tip: Tips on finding and working with a professional book coach by Les Kletke
www.lesthebookcoach.com

It is not so much about finding a book coach – it is a matter of **finding the right one**. There are two primary concerns that make you and your coach a good fit.

The system – some coaches advocate writing down everything you know on the topic of your book and then sorting it into sections, chapters, and paragraphs. And of course editing your *masterpiece* from there. ☺

The other way of doing things is to have a structure in place and to write with a goal in mind. Have a target and structure each of your chapters to move the reader toward that target.

Either system will work, but it is a matter of which fits your personality. It is easier to find a coach that works with your personality than to try and change. Writing requires enough effort without having to go against the grain of your personality throughout the process.

The other prime concern is trust. Is the coach someone you trust entirely?

You are going to (or should be) sharing a lot of information with your coach. You need to be confident in openly sharing information. Some of it will not be included in the book, but your coach may need to know it for background.

Your relationship with your coach will grow through the process, but if you don't have the trust for a solid foundation, it is not going to give you the best final product possible.

You should also consider your coach's history. Not whether they are great writers, but if they have worked with people in similar genres. Often a great writer is not a good coach or editor. Just as in athletics, the most successful coaches have not been great players — they seldom are.

Choose a coach who truly understands the process of writing and can effectively guide you. Don't gauge them by how many bestsellers they have written, rather by how many best sellers their clients have written.

When you choose a book coach you are embarking on a journey with them, a journey that will have some challenges.

A good coach recognizes when you need a (virtual) hug and when you need a kick in the pants and knows the difference. And that difference works!

"When your story is ready for rewrite, cut it to the bone. Get rid of every ounce of excess fat. This is going to hurt; revising a story down to the bare essentials is always a little like murdering children, but it must be done."
Stephen King

Success Publications

Helping translate your ideas and brilliance into pixels and print – you can become a published author today!

If you have ever wanted to write a book, have one in process that you need to publish, or are looking for book coaching, proofreading, formatting and ideas, this is your day, we are here to help. It has never been easier or less expensive to publish - **Now is the Time!** Now is 'your' time to become a successfully published author.

We originally started Success Publications for Bob's books; but have essentially turned it into a Boutique Publishing adventure to assist fellow speakers and authors in their quest to publish.

We can help you reach this dream! www.SuccessPublications.ca
Connect with us: Bob 'Idea Man' Hooey bhooey@mcsnet.ca
Irene Gaudet: igaudet@mcsnet.ca
Creative Office: +1-780-736-0009

We can help with the following: Ask for pricing

- Coaching/consulting
- Proof reading
- Editing
- Layout and Formatting
- Cover Design and development
- Kindle, CreateSpace, Amazon, and Smashwords submissions
- Electronic newsletter or e-zine design and delivery; or design with your supplier
- Graphic design (e.g. logo or webpage header)
- Distribution
- Promotion

Copyright and license notes

WRITE ON! *Idea-rich tips and techniques to bring your book into pixels or print*

Bob 'Idea Man' Hooey, Accredited Speaker, 2011 Spirit of CAPS recipient. Prolific author of 30 plus business, leadership, and career success publications

© Copyright 2020-2023 Bob 'Idea Man' Hooey

Photos of Bob: **Bonnie-Jean McAllister**,
www.elantraphotography.com
Dov Friedman, www.photographybyDov.com
Editorial, layout and design:
Irene Gaudet, Vitrak Creative Services, ww.vitrakcreative.com

ISBN: 9781998014255 IS
Printed in Canada and the United States 10 9 8 7 6 5 4 3 2 1

Success Publications – a division of Creativity Corner Inc.
Box 10, Egremont, AB T0A 0Z0
www.successpublications.ca

Acknowledgements, credits

As with each of my books, a special dedication of this piece of myself, to the two people who meant the most to me, my folks **Ron and Marge Hooey**. Sadly, both my parents left this earthly realm in 1999. I still miss our time together and your encouragement and love. I was blessed with the two of you in my life. I've recently added **George and Lillian Sidor** (Irene's parents) to this list.

To my inspiring wife and professional proof-reader and publications coach, **Irene Gaudet**, who loves, encourages, and supports me in my quest to continue sharing my **Ideas At Work!** across the world. Thank you seems so inadequate for your timely work in helping make my writing and my client service better! I love the time we spend together!

To my colleagues and friends in Toastmasters, the National Speakers Association (NSA), the Canadian Association of Professional Speakers (CAPS), and the Global Speakers Federation (GSF) who continually challenge me to strive for success and increased excellence.

To my great audiences, leaders, students, coaching clients, and readers across the globe who share their experiences and enjoyment of my work. Your positive and supportive feedback encourages me to keep working on additional programs and success publications like this updated version. My experience with you Succeeds the foundation for additional real-life experiences I can take from the stage to the page, the classroom to the boardroom.

My thanks to a select few friends for your ongoing support and 'constructive' abuse. You know who you are. ☺

Disclaimer

Bob's B.E.S.T. publications

Bob is a *prolific* author who has been capturing and sharing his wisdom and experience in print and electronic formats for the past fifteen plus years.

In addition to the following publications, several of them best-sellers, he has written for consumer, corporate, professional associations, trade, and on-line publications.

He has been engaged to write and assist on publications by other best-selling writers and successful companies.

His publications are listed to give you an idea of the scope and topics he writes about. Bob's **B**usiness **E**nhancement **S**uccess **T**ools. **Visit: www.SuccessPublications.ca** for more information and to order your own copies

Leadership, business, and career development series

- **Running TOO Fast** (8th edition 2022)
- **Legacy of Leadership** (6th edition 2024)
- **Make ME Feel Special!** (6th edition 2022)
- **Why Didn't I 'THINK' of That?** (5th edition 2022)
- **Speaking for Success!** (10h edition 2023)
- **THINK Beyond the First Sale** (3rd edition 2022)
- **Prepare Yourself to Win!** (3rd edition 2017)
- **The early years… 1998-2009** – *A Tip of the Hat collection*
- **The saga continues… 2010-2019** - *A Tip of the Hat collection*

Bob's Mini-book success series

- **The Courage to Lead!** (4th edition 2023)
- **Creative Conflict** (3rd edition 2023)

- **Get to YES!** (3rd edition 2023)
- **THINK Before You Ink!** (3rd edition 2023)
- **Running to Win!** (2nd edition 2023)
- **Generate More Sales** (5th edition 2023)
- **Unleash your Business Potential** (3rd edition 2023)
- **Maximize Meetings** (2023)
- **Learn to Listen** (2nd edition 2023)
- **Creativity Counts!** (2nd edition 2023)
- **Create Your Future!** (3rd edition 2023)

Bob's Pocket Wisdom series

- **Pocket Wisdom for Speakers** (updated 2023)
- **Pocket Wisdom for Leaders – Power of One!** (2023)

Kindle Shorts (2017-2023) - more to come in 2024

- **LEAD!** *Idea-rich leadership success strategies*
- **CREATE!** *Idea-rich strategies for enhanced innovation*
- **TIME!** *Idea-rich tips for enhanced performance and productivity*
- **SERVE!** *Idea-rich strategies for enhanced customer service*
- **SPEAK!** *Idea-rich tips and techniques for great presentations*
- **CREATIVE CONFLICT** *Idea-rich leadership for team success*
- **SUCCEED!** *Idea-rich strategies to succeed in business, despite global disruptions (2020)*
- **WRITE ON!** *Idea-rich tips and techniques to bring your book into pixels or print (2020)*

Co-authored books created by Bob

- Quantum Success – 3 volume series (2006)
- **In the Company of Leaders** (95th anniversary 2019)
- Foundational Success (2nd Edition 2013)

What they say about Bob 'Idea Man' Hooey

I frequently travel across North America, and more recently around the globe, sharing my **Ideas At Work!**

I am fortunate to get feedback and comments from my audiences and colleagues. These comments come from people who have been touched, challenged, or enjoyed themselves in my sessions.

"I still get comments from people about your presentation. Only a few speakers have left an impression that lasts that long. You hit a spot with the tourism people." **Janet Bell**, Yukon Economic Forums

*"**Thank you, Bob**, it is always a pleasure to see a true professional at work. You have made the name 'Speaker' stand out as a truism - someone who encourages people to examine their lives and adjust. The comments indicated you hit people right where it is important - in their hearts. Each of those in your audience took away a new feeling of personal success and encouragement."* **Sherry Knight**, Dimension Eleven Human Resources and Communications

*"On very short notice Bob cleared his schedule and graciously presented at our meeting when the original Speaker was unable to attend. **Last week Bob set the tone for our two-day BMO leadership meeting and gave us all a motivational lift.** His compassion and true interest in people was clearly evident, making him very credible. He shared some great stories, has a wealth of experience and knowledge and it was a pleasure listening to him. His down-to-Earth style makes it easier to retain the information presented. He also followed up with additional info and handouts, cementing his message of building bridges, not walls. Fantastic job, Bob, and thanks again!"* **Barbara Afra Beler**, MBA, Senior Specialist Commercial Community, Alberta North

"I have been so excited working with Bob Hooey, as he has given inspiration and motivation to our leadership team members. Both at the Brick Warehouse – Alberta and at Art Van Furniture – Michigan; with his years of experience in working with business executives and his humorous and delightful packaging of his material, he makes learning with Bob a real joy. But most importantly, anyone who encounters his material is the better for it." **Kim Yost**, retired CEO Art Van Furniture, former CEO The Brick

Motivate your teams, your employees, and your leaders to 'productively' grow and 'profitably' succeed!

Protect your conference investment - leverage your training dollars.

Enhance your professional career and sell more products and services.

Equip and motivate your leaders and their teams to grow and succeed, 'even' in tough times!

Leverage your time to enhance your skills, equip your teams, and better serve your clients.

Leverage your leadership and investment of time to leave a significant legacy!

Call today to engage best-selling author, award winning, inspirational leadership keynote speaker, leaders' success coach, and employee development trainer, **Bob 'Idea Man' Hooey** and his innovative, audience based, results-focused, **Ideas At Work!** for your next company, convention, leadership, staff, training, or association event. You'll be glad you did!

Call +1-780-736-0009 to connect with Bob 'Idea Man' Hooey today! Email: bhooey@mcsnet.ca Learn more about Bob at: **www.ideaman.net** or **www.BobHooey.training**

"In challenging times people need HELP and they need HOPE! That, is MY business!" Bob 'Idea Man' Hooey

To succeed in 'any' business or creative endeavor is an elusive quest, but an attainable one. You can do it! **More than ever,** amidst this global disruption, we need to reassess what business we are in, who are our potential clients, and how can we best reach and serve them despite these challenging times.

Those who take this seriously and adapt will emerge stronger, perhaps, totally redesigned and restructured. And, more relevant and profitable as well. **This is our opportunity**, our challenge, as business leaders, to demonstrate our commitment to our clients, teams, suppliers, and communities. **As authors**, we can choose our words to define our future growth and success.

We can do it by working together!

Canada's IdeaMan, Bob Hooey partners with committed leaders, organizations and fellow communicators to equip and motivate for profitable growth and success. He teaches secrets of idea-rich business and leadership development built on solid foundations and taking strategic action.

Bob is the prolific author of business, career, and leadership success books (over 30 in all) and travels the world sharing his innovative Ideas at Work!

WRITE ON! *Idea-rich tips and techniques to bring your book into pixels or print*

Success Publications
ISBN: 9781998014255 Ingram Spark edition